Origami
Bugs

Catherine Ard

Gareth Stevens
PUBLISHING

Please visit our website, www.garethstevens.com. For a free color catalog of all our high-quality books, call toll free 1-800-542-2595 or fax 1-877-542-2596.

Library of Congress Cataloging-in-Publication Data
Ard, Catherine.
Origami bugs / by Catherine Ard.
p. cm. — (Amazing origami)
Includes index.
ISBN 978-1-4824-2256-6 (pbk.)
ISBN 978-1-4824-2257-3 (6-pack)
ISBN 978-1-4824-2199-6 (library binding)
1. Origami – Juvenile literature. 2. Insects in art – Juvenile literature. I. Title.
TT870.A73 2015
736.982—d23

First Edition

Published in 2015 by
Gareth Stevens Publishing
111 East 14th Street, Suite 349
New York, NY 10003

Copyright © 2015 Arcturus Publishing

Models and photography: Michael Wiles
Text: Catherine Ard
Design: Emma Randall and Belinda Webster
Editor: Joe Harris
Bug photography: Shutterstock

Printed in the United States of America

CPSIA compliance information: Batch CW15GS: For further information contact
Gareth Stevens, New York, New York at 1-800-542-2595.

Contents

Basic folds

Origami has been popular in Japan for hundreds of years and is now loved all around the world. You can make great models with just one sheet of paper... and this book shows you how!

The paper used in origami is thin but strong, so that it can be folded many times. It is usually colored on one side. Alternatively, you can use ordinary scrap paper, but make sure it's not too thick.

Origami models often share the same folds and basic designs. This introduction explains some of the folds that you will need for the projects in this book. When making the models, follow the key below to find out what the lines and arrows mean. And always crease well!

KEY

valley fold ‐ ‐ ‐ ‐ ‐ ‐ ‐ ‐ ‐ ‐ ‐ ‐ ‐ ‐ ‐
step fold (mountain and valley fold next to each other)
direction to move paper

mountain fold • • • • • • • • • • • • • • •
push ▼

MOUNTAIN FOLD

To make a mountain fold, fold the paper so that the crease is pointing up towards you, like a mountain.

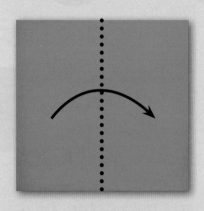
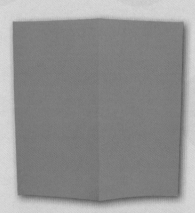

VALLEY FOLD

To make a valley fold, fold the paper the other way, so that the crease is pointing away from you, like a valley.

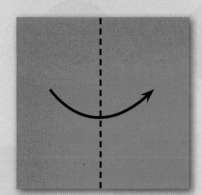

INSIDE REVERSE FOLD

An inside reverse fold is useful if you want to make a nose or a tail, or if you want to flatten off the shape of another part of an origami model.

① Practice by first folding a piece of paper diagonally in half. Make a valley fold on one point and crease.

② It's important to make sure that the paper is creased well. Run your finger over the crease two or three times.

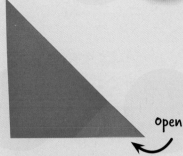

③ Unfold and open up the corner slightly. Refold the crease nearest to you into a mountain fold.

④ Open up the paper a little more and then tuck the tip of the point inside. Close the paper. This is the view from the underside of the paper.

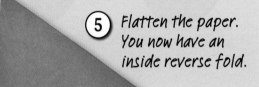

⑤ Flatten the paper. You now have an inside reverse fold.

OUTSIDE REVERSE FOLD

An outside reverse fold is useful if you want to make a head, beak, or foot, or another part of your model that sticks out.

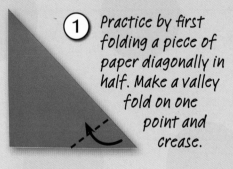

① Practice by first folding a piece of paper diagonally in half. Make a valley fold on one point and crease.

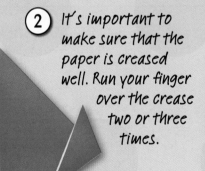

② It's important to make sure that the paper is creased well. Run your finger over the crease two or three times.

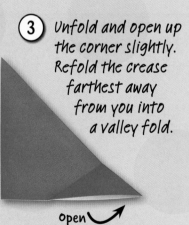

③ Unfold and open up the corner slightly. Refold the crease farthest away from you into a valley fold.

④ Open up the paper a little more and start to turn the corner inside out. Then close the paper when the fold begins to turn.

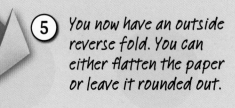

⑤ You now have an outside reverse fold. You can either flatten the paper or leave it rounded out.

Ladybug

Ladybugs are not always red. Some ladybugs are orange, yellow, black, brown, or pink. Here's how to fold a cute red ladybug. You just need to add the spots!

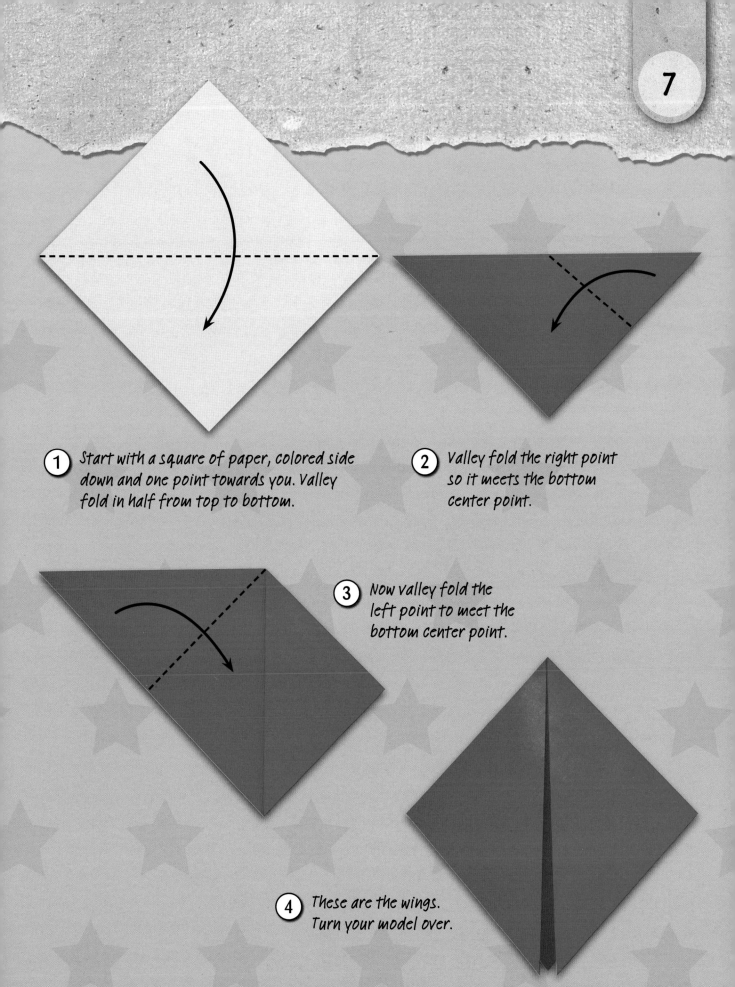

1. Start with a square of paper, colored side down and one point towards you. Valley fold in half from top to bottom.

2. Valley fold the right point so it meets the bottom center point.

3. Now valley fold the left point to meet the bottom center point.

4. These are the wings. Turn your model over.

5 Valley fold the top corner down.

6 Mountain fold the flap back.

7 Valley fold the right corner.

8 Valley fold the left corner.

Did You Know?

Different types of ladybugs have different numbers of spots. Some have only two spots, while others have 24 spots… or more!

9 Valley fold the top point down.

10 Turn your model over.

11 Your ladybug is ready to fly! Decorate her wings with black spots.

Cicada

In warm countries, the sound of cicadas chirping fills the night air in spring and summer. This origami version is fun to fold and not nearly so noisy!

1. Start with a square of paper, colored side down and one point towards you. Valley fold in half from bottom to top.

2. Valley fold the right point to meet the top point.

3. Now valley fold the left point up to meet the top center point.

4. Valley fold the top right flap down.

Did You Know?

Cicadas can spend up to 17 years living underground. When they finally come above ground they only live for about five weeks.

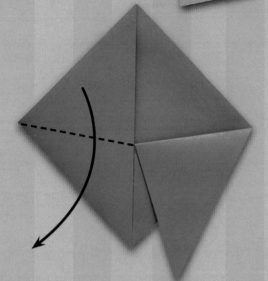

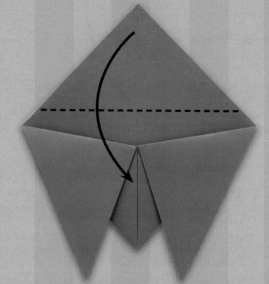

5 Do the same on the other side. You now have two wings.

6 Valley fold the top layer of the top point.

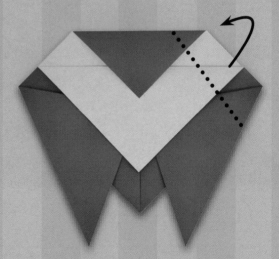

7 Now valley fold the bottom layer about 1/2 inch (15 mm) above the fold you just made.

8 Mountain fold the right side.

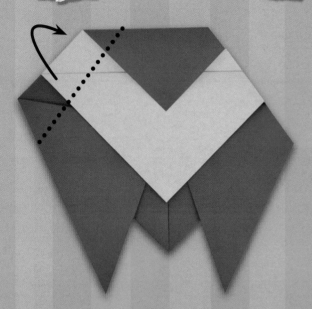

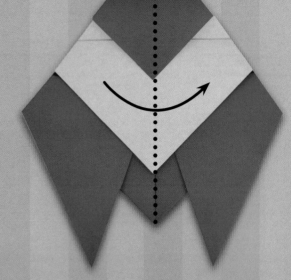

9. Mountain fold the left side.

10. Mountain fold the paper in half from left to right, then unfold.

11. Draw two eyes on the head and sit your striped cicada up on its neatly folded wings.

Stag beetle

Stag beetles get their name from their gigantic jaws, which look like the antlers on a stag. They use their jaws to wrestle rival stag beetles, not to hurt humans!

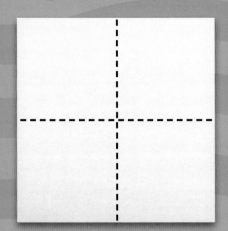

1. Colored side facing down, fold the paper from top to bottom and unfold, then from left to right and unfold.

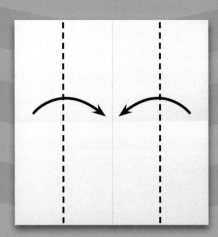

2. Valley fold the sides to meet the center crease.

3. Now valley fold the top and bottom edges to meet in the center.

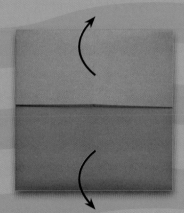

4. Open out the folds you made in step 3.

5. Valley fold the top corners to meet the first crease from the top.

6. Unfold the corners.

Did You Know?

Stag beetle larvae are good for your garden because they eat up lots of rotting wood, but never touch living plants.

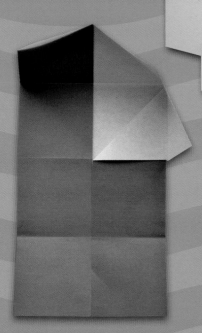

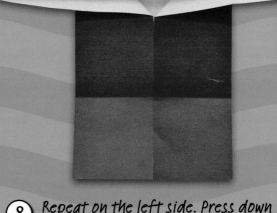

(7) Open up the top layer on the right and fold it down to meet the center crease.

(8) Repeat on the left side. Press down on the top to flatten the paper.

(9) Valley fold the points to make two new triangles. Their points should stick straight up.

(10) These points make the beetle's "antlers." Turn the paper over.

(11) Fold in the bottom section along the crease, as shown.

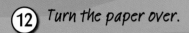

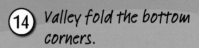

12 Turn the paper over.

13 Fold in the sides, lining them up with the inside edges of the triangles.

14 Valley fold the bottom corners.

15 Turn the model over.

16 Draw two beady black eyes near the top edge. Now your origami stag beetle is ready for battle!

Butterfly

Butterflies have four delicate wings, often covered with colorful patterns. Follow the steps to make a beautiful butterfly, ready to flutter to the next flower.

① Colored side facing down, valley fold the paper diagonally one way and unfold, then the other way.

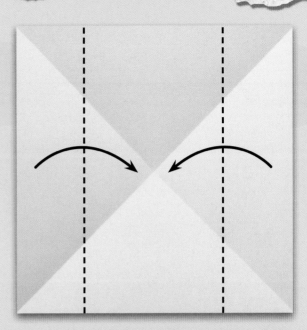

② Unfold the paper. Valley fold the sides to meet the center.

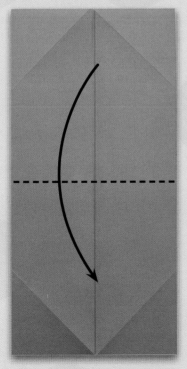

③ Fold in half and unfold.

④ Valley fold the top and bottom to meet the center.

⑤ Open up the top section.

⑥ Take the top layer and pull out the corners. Press down on the top to flatten the paper.

⑦ You should now have this shape. Unfold the bottom section.

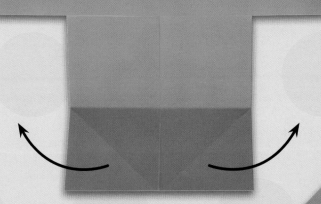

⑧ Repeat step 5 with the other corners.

⑨ Fold down the bottom right flap.

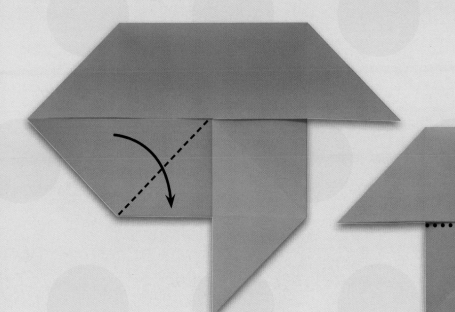

⑩ Do the same on the other side.

⑪ Mountain fold the top section behind the bottom section.

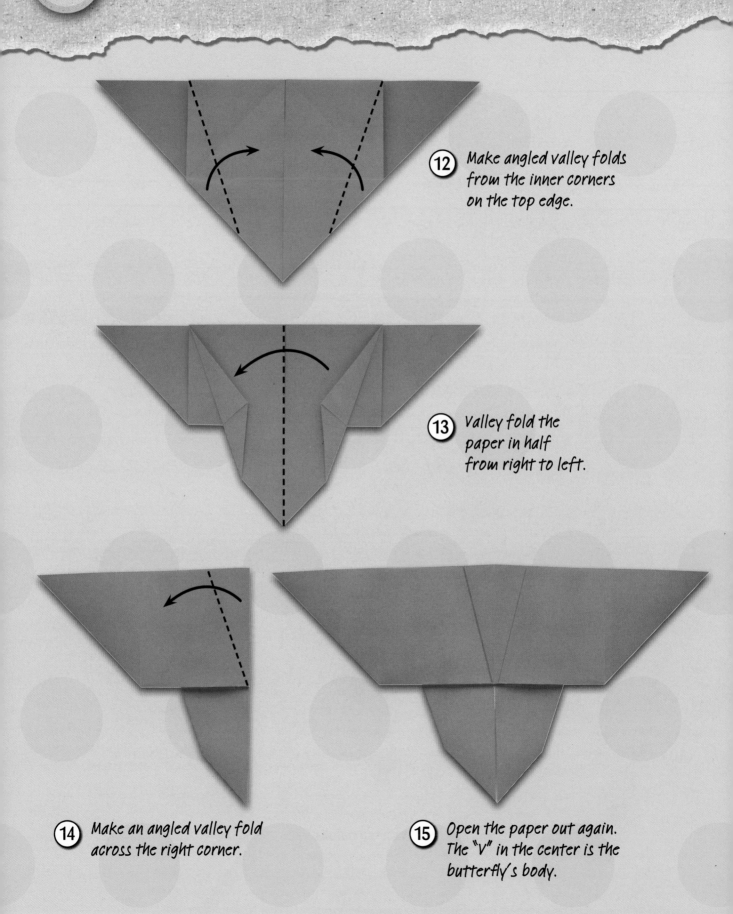

12 Make angled valley folds from the inner corners on the top edge.

13 Valley fold the paper in half from right to left.

14 Make an angled valley fold across the right corner.

15 Open the paper out again. The "V" in the center is the butterfly's body.

16 To make the body stick out, fold the left side across the right along the new crease.

17 Repeat with the right side.

18 Your fluttery butterfly is finished. You could add some pretty wing patterns to bring it to life!

24 Bumblebee

Medium

Bumblebees are known for their bold stripes and fuzzy bodies. Get busy folding this friendly insect from yellow paper, then draw its black stripes with a pen.

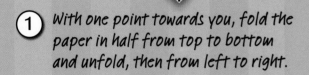

1 With one point towards you, fold the paper in half from top to bottom and unfold, then from left to right.

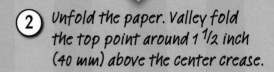

2 Unfold the paper. Valley fold the top point around 1 ½ inch (40 mm) above the center crease.

3 Mountain fold the right corner, lining up the colored edge with the center crease on the reverse.

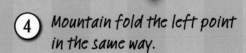

4 Mountain fold the left point in the same way.

5 Valley fold the left and right corners as shown.

Did You Know?

A bumblebee needs to warm up before takeoff. It does this by shivering – just like we do when we are cold!

6 Your paper should look like this. Unfold the right flap.

7 Valley fold the corner tip so the edge meets the crease you made in step 5.

8 Unfold the left flap.

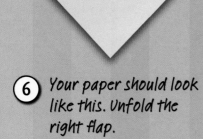

9 Valley fold the corner tip so the edge meets the crease you made in step 5.

10 Unfold the right flap and open up the corner. Press it flat to make a triangle.

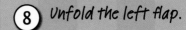

(11) Now do the same thing with the left flap.

(12) Valley fold the top point.

(13) Turn your model over.

(14) Stick on two round eyes and draw black stripes across the body. Your brilliant bumblebee is complete!

Caterpillar

Caterpillars nibble juicy leaves all day long! All that munching makes them big and strong, ready to change from a creepy-crawly into a fluttery butterfly or moth.

1. With the paper colored side down and one point towards you, make a valley fold 2 3/4 inch (70 mm) from the top.

2. Now valley fold the bottom corner so that the point meets the top edge.

3. Turn the paper over.

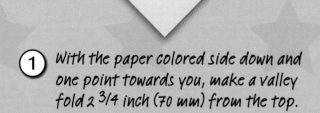

4. Make a step fold on the right point. This is the caterpillar's tail.

5. Make another step fold about 1 1/4 inch (30 mm) from the folded edge.

6 Make another step fold, keeping the folds an even distance apart.

7 Continue with another step fold.

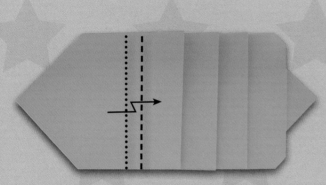

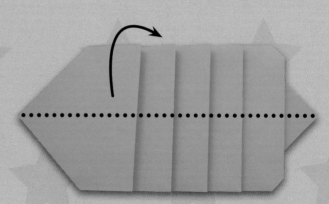

8 Make a final step fold. These folds are the sections of the caterpillar's body.

9 Mountain fold the paper in half.

Did You Know?

A caterpillar has as many as 4,000 muscles in its tiny, wriggly body. The human body only has 629 muscles.

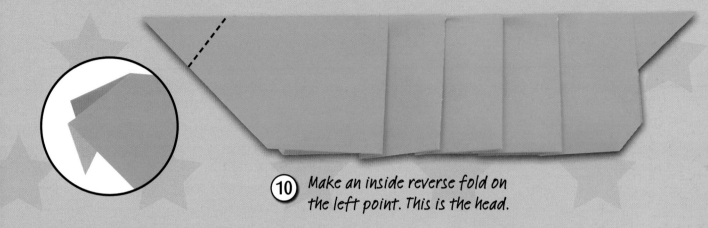

10 Make an inside reverse fold on the left point. This is the head.

11 Hold either end of the caterpillar between your fingers and gently pull apart to give the body a curved shape.

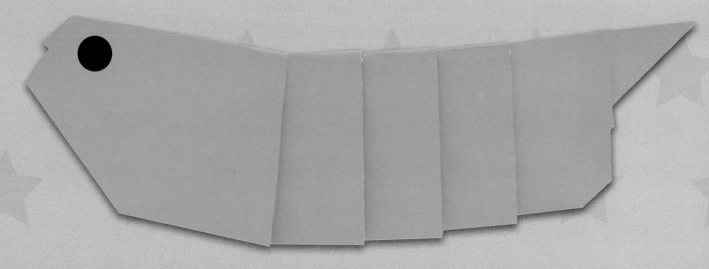

12 Finish by drawing an eye on either side of the head. Now place your origami caterpillar on a plant or a paper leaf ready to munch some lunch!

Glossary

antlers Horns shaped like branches that grow out of the head of a deer.

crease A line in a piece of paper made by folding.

delicate Easily damaged.

jaws The mouthparts used for grasping, biting or crushing.

larvae The young of an insect or animal that have left their eggs but are not yet fully grown.

mountain fold An origami step where a piece of paper is folded so that the crease is pointing upwards, like a mountain.

nectar A sugary liquid produced by flowers.

rival A person or creature competing for the same area or thing.

sap The watery fluid that flows inside plants and trees.

step fold A mountain fold and valley fold next to each other.

valley fold An origami step where a piece of paper is folded so that the crease is pointing downwards, like a valley.

Further Reading

Akass, Susan. *My First Origami Book*. Cico Kidz, 2011.

Biddle, Steve & Megumi Biddle. *Paper Capers*. Dover Publications, 2014.

Ono, Mari & Hiroaki Takai. *Dinogami*. Cico Books, 2012.

Robinson, Nick & Susan Behar. *Origami XOXO*. Ivy Press, 2012.

Index